BETWEEN
ME & DAD

The 7 Powers to Healing and Freedom
A Companion Journal

by

CHARLES HOLT

Charles Holt Productions, LLC
Los Angeles, California

Published by Charles Holt Productions, LLC
8033 Sunset Boulevard
Suite 167
Los Angeles, CA 90046
213-309-2615
www.betweenmeanddad.com

Distributed by Charles Holt Productions, LLC
www.charlesholtproductions.com

Between Me and Dad
The 7 Powers to Healing and Freedom
A Companion Journal
Charles Holt

Editor: Kuwana Haulsey
Book Cover and Interior Design: Pip Abrigo
Executive in Charge of Publication: Charles Holt

Printed in USA on recycled paper

ISBN: 978-0-692-24942-0

Contents

Introduction • *1*

Power One: • *5*
The Power of Release

Power Two: • *14*
The Power of Remembrance

Power Three: • *23*
The Power of Self Discovery

Power Four: • *32*
The Power of Compassion

Power Five: • *42*
The Power of Surrender

Power Six: • *52*
The Power of Authentic Integrity

Power Seven: • *61*
The Power of You

Introduction

When I was a little boy, maybe about four or five years old, I remember fidgeting and squirming under my mother's watchful eye. She wanted me to sit still. I was trying, but there was so much to do—so much fun to be had. And I was missing out on all of it.

"Son," my mother said, "Stop tapping your foot." I heard her, but of course I still kept tapping. After a moment, I heard my father's powerful voice scold, "Didn't she tell you to stop?" As soon as he said the words, I stopped what I was doing and sat up straight, tall and quiet. At that time, my reaction to my father wasn't a sign of fear. It was reverence. When my father spoke, I listened.

A father brings a certain type of energy to a household. He exudes order and security. The power of fatherhood rests in the ability of his male energy to lead the way on the path toward healthy, sustainable living. His presence then becomes a demonstration of manhood for the impressionable young eyes watching his every move. When we don't have that demonstration, we move through life like scattered pieces of fabric. It becomes extremely difficult to connect with anything or anyone or to set healthy boundaries. And you know that if you don't set boundaries to a piece of fabric, sooner or later it comes undone. Then all we have left are a bunch of frayed, disconnected pieces. In our lives, those pieces are called pain. They're called the disconnection of communication. They're called poignant disappointment. We find ourselves wondering what on earth we did to cause the pain that we're experiencing.

So what happens to the young men, myself included, who didn't naturally develop healthy, loving relationships with the men who sired them? What happens to the men who were forced to grow up without any contact with their father whatsoever? Missing out on this crucial piece of one's self can lead to a life of pain, resentment and missed opportunities. It can also lead us to unconsciously repeat the cycle of abandonment with our own children. That cycle of pain, shame, blame and resentment must be broken.

This book is a conduit for creating a new level of consciousness in your life and an even greater understanding of what's possible on your healing journey. It's a companion journal based on the teachings in my book *Between Me and Dad*, which goes into great depths about the journey to healing and wholeness. True healing requires letting go of past hurts and false beliefs. This book aims to help you do both—heal the past and look toward the future, while standing in the present. When you can do that you become an example. You realize that you matter. What you say, feel and do matters to the world.

A person's perception of his self-worth can be badly damaged when a primary caregiver doesn't fulfill his role. But real self worth cannot be touched by the actions or inactions of another. Throughout my life, my mother told me that I was worthy. So did everyone else around me, with the exception of my father. But the building of my mental, emotional and spiritual house didn't begin until I started to explore and discover who I was for myself.

My hope is that this book can be a companion to you as you head down the healing path yourself. I want this book to be accessible to anyone who's ever felt the sting of loss or abandonment or disconnection from his father. Some of you may have had an experience similar to my own: you grew up with a father who was physically present in the home, but who was mentally and emotionally absent. Others may never have lived with their father in the home, and still others might never even have met the man. He was like a ghost, rarely spoken of and never seen. Whatever the circumstance, we're all left trying to figure out that crucial relationship—the good, the bad and the awful. We're left with so many questions tangled up in our minds that we don't know how to get past them.

But that's the catch: we must first make it through this entanglement before we can truly start to live our life's purpose. Though it's difficult, it can be done. The process is systematic. We have to start putting the pieces together on a day-by-day, and sometimes moment-by-moment, basis. We must become conscious of our thoughts, beliefs, fears and triggers, as well as our desires and dreams. We want to create such momentum that the desire for transformation becomes a continuum in our consciousness. And we won't let it go because it won't let us go.

A continuum of self-discovery and the creation of self-worth are the foundation for building our own house; we understand in a new and deeper way that what we say matters, what we do matters and how we move about in the world matters. At the end of the day, we're led to ask the question: *what's really important to me?* And then we begin to take the inward journey of finding out.

To be clear, we don't need the approval of our fathers, or whoever it was that disappointed us, to access our good. This journey may lead some of us toward reconciliation with our fathers. Some of us, however, will never have that experience. Either way, it's all good. Our healing doesn't depend on the outcome of that relationship. Speaking for myself, I'm grateful that my father remained on this earth long enough for us to make amends. But to tell the truth, I've had more than my fair share of "I wish" stories. I wish we could have sat down and talked sooner. *I wish he could've come to my baseball games. I wish my father would've taken me to church.* Now, he's gone. So what do I do? I wish upon my own star. And I look at the positive examples that I did have.

I'm glad I saw my father put pennies in their paper wrappers to save. He taught me the value of money. I'm glad that my father said, "It's not what you get, it's what you take care of." As a result, I've learned how to take care of my car, my clothes and all of the little things that I've been blessed with that I might otherwise have taken for granted. Though we didn't get along for most of my life, my father gave me the opportunity to understand what it means to be grateful, and to be a good steward. I even understand my relationships with my friends on a deeper level. My dad always said that friends come and go. He said, "They might be here with you ten years and all of a sudden they say they don't want to be your friend anymore. Or maybe you don't want to be their friend and they go. But it's important to make sure that while you are friends, you're the best friend they got! That's what a friend is."

My father taught me some very valuable lessons about holding onto other people's promises.

What he actually said to me was, "You don't even hold onto your own promises. How you going to hold onto somebody else's?"

As I child, I couldn't understand why he said some of the things that he said, especially because some of it landed so hard. But I understand the intention behind his words now, so I'm able to celebrate now.

We're living in an accelerated time in terms of the upleveling of our collective consciousness. As technology accelerates, we accelerate too. If we look around us, we can see that even nature is constantly accelerating in balancing and healing itself. Our consciousness also has the ability to try and heal itself at an accelerated rate. We don't have to wait until we're forty or fifty or sixty to get it. We can get it regardless of where we are.

It doesn't matter what somebody else has said to (or about) you. It doesn't matter what your bank account looks like. And it doesn't matter whether your father was unavailable to you growing up. This is a whole new world. It's a whole new opportunity to get things in order. I do realize that we're sometimes so beaten down that accessing the impulse to dream feels like pulling teeth. But if you can find the courage to wish upon a star, make a wish for yourself, for your year, right now. I'm not talking about the year that begins on January 1st. I'm talking about your year beginning right now. This is a new beginning. Every day, every moment, is a new beginning. And you get to declare it.

Power One: **The Power of Release**

The power of release is in allowing whatever you're holding the other person hostage over to be dissolved in your mind. This is where we begin to recreate and restructure ourselves and our relationships. Instead of thinking about those negative actions from the past, we sit down and talk about them (if not with our fathers, then with another person we trust). This helps to release the congealed thoughts that we have in our minds that are not the truth and that are based on a circumstance or situation that we've embellished.

The power of release is one of the cornerstones in the foundation of true healing. Being able to release gives us new options. All too often, we accumulate information about our situations or circumstances that then cements our opinions around these "facts." The stories, dramas and embellished beliefs in our minds take on a life of their own. We can set the table for release by understanding that when we learn how to navigate these situations and conditions, they will no longer be able to run our lives.

We must learn how to look at a situation and see the lesson in it. And then, after the lesson has been revealed, we can allow the emotional charge around the situation to be released from having control over our thoughts, actions and deeds. Basically, at the end of the day we want to learn how to let go of things that no longer serve our continued evolution and our goal of becoming more of the good of who we are, without having burdens and barriers in our minds.

When the mind gets going on a certain subject, it fills in details and makes assumptions about what's *really* going on. That's what I call embellishment. We start with a thought as simple as *he didn't like me.* Then we add, *he doesn't like me because I'm black.* That sounds true, so we go a little further and say to ourselves, *he doesn't like me because I intimidated him.* In reality, we don't know if the person likes us or not. But we've just created an entire scenario in our minds. What we choose to believe has its own way of creating a spiral effect. Eventually we'll begin to act out these scenarios in our everyday lives.

We can stop doing that by catching ourselves when we want to go into these types of mental tirades. The people that we've pre-judged have nothing to do with what we've conjured up. They're just backdrops onto which we project our anger and disappointment.

Part of learning to release is recognizing when we've made things up in our minds. If you catch yourself doing this, stop and ask yourself: *where did this belief come from?* Everything has an origin. Then ask yourself: why does it affect me so much? *Why does it keep coming to my attention?*

You can write down your answers or just think about them. Use whatever method works best to assist you in staying conscious in the moment. Conscious self-reflection is the most surefire way to short-circuit unhealthy and unhelpful thoughts. We'll be coming back to this technique again and again throughout this book.

If you choose to write your insights down and create some kind of diary, log or journal, that's great! Keep it handy, where you can visit it often throughout this process. I guarantee that you'll be encouraged by what you find. For some men, it can be just as effective to simply tell themselves to stop the mental chatter. Other people like myself have an *aha moment* where they immediately say, "let me put this into practice." We all learn how to deal with these situations differently.

So, for example, if you find yourself having negative, angry thoughts about something that your father did or didn't do for you (either in the recent or distant past), try to short-circuit the thoughts before engaging in a full-blown mental tirade. Take a step back in your mind. Look at the situation—and your feelings about the situation—

for what it is. Then stop and take a take a deep breath.

When these tirades of thoughts are having their way with us, there's something about the breathing pattern that becomes rapid. Our breathing affects the way that our bodies regulate themselves. So take slow, deep breaths and go to your center. From there, it becomes possible to make conscious choices, rather than rehashing old assumptions and beliefs. That is one of the first vital steps on the journey of self-discovery and healing.

True release has in it the capacity to not hold onto anything. That means releasing expectation, too. When we talk about the power of release we're talking about something that serves as a tributary to self-discovery. So as we move into the power of release we know that it is guiding us yet further into the truth or who we are. We don't need to manipulate or concoct some kind of clever thing to get somebody to agree with us or act a certain way.

Releasing expectation is crucial as we move forward on a path of spiritual and emotional healing. When we release expectation we're basically stating that we don't have to be a prisoner of someone else's actions, or what someone else says or thinks about us. As we continue this process, we're also releasing all of our old thoughts and beliefs about ourselves. When a child's father doesn't show up for him, it's very common for that child to believe that the father's shortcomings and poor choices are a reflection of something that's wrong with him. The child wants the situation to change. He wants to be loved and accepted unconditionally. And, deep in his heart, he *expects* his father to show up for him, to make everything all right. When that doesn't happen disappointment (and sometimes despair) sets in, coloring how he sees his father, the world around him, and even himself.

As the child grows into manhood, those congealed thoughts and beliefs continue to exert control over his life in many ways. What car he drives, where he lives, what he does for a living all reflect the thoughts that he's been holding about himself, both the negative and positive. We can shuffle off those beliefs and redefine who we are. The people that we love and trust can help in this process, but at the end of the day we're ultimately responsible for the way that we show up in the world, which is a direct result of the way that we feel about ourselves.

When we don't have relationships with our fathers releasing the expectation of developing that relationship can be extremely difficult. It's probably one of the most difficult situations to release. When we come out of the womb, we're trying to connect with the people around us right away. Our survival depends on it. When we see and interact with the same caregivers every single day it creates a sense of security for us as infants. It also creates an innate friendship. The possibility of those relationships not adding up the way we feel they should is heartbreaking.

Healing from that kind of disappointment is not a one-shot deal. We don't just say, *OK, we're over it now.* We never get over it. But there are ways for us to learn how to navigate the pain. This can't ensure that the pain never shows up again. We're simply learning how to release any suppressed grief in a way that is empowering and healthy for ourselves and our present relationships.

Release continues to nurture encouragement. It's not easy to take the first step. But when you release what you've been holding, your heart opens. You've opened another portal into your own soul. That takes courage. Having the courage to release begets more courage and even greater release. You begin to let go of all manner of things that you've been holding onto. Then you begin to release you. You come to the understanding that you're all right with the parts of yourself that have been hindering you and you allow them to leave gracefully, gratefully, and without judgment.

Would you agree that releasing old habits, thoughts and ways of being give you an opportunity to live a better life? (I invite you to speak aloud the sacred "yes" in agreement here). Even when we understand the benefits of letting go of the past, it's not easy to take the first step in that process. It takes great courage to say, *I'm ready to let go of those things that have been hindering me; I'm ready to grow.* Quite often, growth requires a pruning process; the things, ideas and people that we've outgrown fall away from us.

Stepping into the sacred "yes", activating the principle called courage, provides us with momentum on our healing journey. It continues to give us insight in taking the next step. It gets us to ask the question, *where do I go now?* Having the courage to move forward keeps us from getting stuck. Let me tell you, we all get stuck. That's the common denominator of moving forward. One of the things that allows for us to release ourselves from being stuck is recognizing that most of the time we're stuck in our minds.

When something seems to be an obstacle another way to move around it is to ask questions about how to release the situation or circumstance and allow it to move itself out of our way. Instead of pushing or shoving or manipulating, instead of trying to step over or on top of it, we can simply allow our roadblocks to move themselves out of our path.

For example you may be in a relationship that has timed out and needs to be released, but you don't want to do it. However you know that in order to move on, you have to let the person go—whether it be a friend, mate or your father. So what do you do? You look at how the relationship has served you and ask the question: *why am I still so adamant about being in the relationship?* Oftentimes we get into relationships because we think that the relationship will give us something that will complete us. But if were on this journey of self-discovery and healing and release, the foundation that we're establishing will allow us to recognize that we're complete within ourselves. This is the power in the process of self-inquiry.

Believe it or not, another tool that we can use to delve further into the art of release is exercise. When we feel better about our bodies we think better thoughts about our environment and the people in it. We certainly think better thoughts about ourselves because some part of us is in action and is becoming better. That's one thing that we can do in terms of getting clarity on whatever situations we may find ourselves in.

Another great thing to do is to go on a pleasure hunt, where you seek out things and activities to get your mind off of any unhealthy situations that must be healed. This isn't avoidance; it's taking a moment of reprieve, a deep breath. Do something you enjoy. If that's roller-skating or going out into nature and taking a walk, do it. Meditate on the beauty of nature, and how the natural world will always heal itself. We can begin to intuit the wisdom of the trees and know that if we look carefully enough, we'll find the same wisdom within ourselves. Sometimes, how we see a tree is also a reflection of how we see ourselves.

Another thing you can do is go to a movie. Go to a movie that you wouldn't normally watch and see how it resonates with you. As we give ourselves liberty to step out of our comfort zone we'll find that we've moved into a land of possibility much quicker than we would have if we'd stayed settled where we were, thinking that our problems would eventually go away by themselves. They will not. Have no doubt, your problems will go away, but you have to release them. Release is an action word. It's not a noun. You must be a participant in your own unfoldment.

Take a Breath

Let's stop right here and take a breath. Think about this healing journey that we're on and embrace it in your heart. When you take on something new—it doesn't matter what it is—the first thing that you do is take a breath to get ready. That breath allows your anxiety to be released.

As we make the conscious effort to release, many things can come up to block our path. Fear that the process won't work often comes up. We may say to ourselves, *I've tried this before.* Fear of failure can also come up. There may be anxiety around what people will think about you, particularly your father, if he's still around. These things will come up because you're going to change if you stick with this process. Your mind is going to change. You're going to change the way you see things and you're going to change the way you see yourself. So whenever you feel that something is going to try to keep you holding onto old beliefs from the past, stop and take a breath. Then ask your self the question: *what is important to me now?*

If you can state what's important to you, it will call forth order in your life. Order gets us into setting healthy boundaries. As we grow, the boundaries get larger. Take a few minutes to write the answer to the question *what is important to me now?* Write in the space below or use extra space in your journal if necessary.

_____
_____
_____
_____
_____
_____
_____
_____

Affirmation

Form a personal affirmation based on your answer to the question above. Write out the affirmation in the space below. Go look in the mirror and see yourselves as you state the affirmation.

_____

_____

_____

_____

Questions and Answers

How will the release of old things allow my life to be better? How will the release of old beliefs allow my life to be better? How does release in general allow me to live a better life?

_____

_____

_____

_____

_____

_____

_____

_____

_____

_____

_____

_____

_____

_____

_____

_____

_____

_____

_____

Power Two:
The Power of Remembrance

Remembering gives us an opportunity to look at ourselves, where we are and where we've been, and encounter our own growth. We give ourselves another point of reference for the pain that we've experienced. We get to examine what that pain really meant for us at that time and to be honest about what still resonates with us. Most importantly, it gives us an opportunity to ask questions like, "Why is it still so painful?" "How can I resolve it?" "How can I get past it this time?"

As we release the sting of past hurts and move toward having a new perspective, this is one of the key things to remember: don't run away when confronted with old pain. Don't think that something is wrong with you because you're having these feelings of sadness or disappointment or anger. Look at what's triggering these feelings and ask yourself: *why is this person (or situation or thought) making me angry?* If you're still being triggered by something that happened long ago, you might ask, *why is it lingering with me?*

At the end of the release section I asked if you agreed that release would give you the opportunity to live a better life. If you said yes, or even if you said no (particularly if you said no), please understand that this process is going to somehow become bigger than life itself. Most people get stuck in the beginning, but this is temporary. Remembrance gives us an opportunity to look at ourselves and once again see where we are and where we've come from so that we can encounter our growth. Believe it or not, this makes it much easier to then go ahead and release those memories and past pains.

As we grow up and become adults, the memories of our encounters with our fathers help form both our worldview and personal narrative. They are part of the emotional collage that shapes our perception of our experiences. These memories are the raw materials from which we construct a mental landscape of what we've come through, how we've handled things and how we've mishandled things, so to speak. It gives us a good barometer on how we've grown.

However, we can also choose to give ourselves a new frame of reference for many of the pains that we've experienced, particularly the pain of fatherlessness. Delving into painful memories can feel counterintuitive because most of the time these are exactly the incidents and situations that we don't want to remember. If we've been neglected, abandoned or abused by our fathers, it's much easier to bury the memories deep inside the subconscious mind. But acknowledging the legacy of the past helps us move through the cycle of pain.

Somewhere along the line, the bullying thoughts regarding our pains and traumas became too painful. So we hid them away in order to continue to function in our day-to-day lives. Acknowledgment gives us a starting point where we can begin to take power over experiences where we may have felt powerless.

After acknowledging whatever uncomfortable thoughts or memories arise, we go back into self-inquiry. We might ask: *how does this memory make me feel now? Do I want this to stay like it is? Do I want to continue to allow this to be a part of the way that I live?* If your answer is yes, then you will continue to allow your memories to run your life. But if you're ready to shift how these memories make you feel, you'll stand and face them. Being with those painful memories doesn't mean settling into annihilation. But you do want to let the memories run their course so you can see them for what they really are.

Without going through this process, your painful memories will remain hindrances, not steppingstones. People want to find different ways to maneuver around their memories or manipulate them as they attempt to climb into their greater good. But the memories become like quicksand. The ego will try to fool us into thinking that we're moving or gaining ground when we're really sinking.

The point of empowerment is in finding healthy ways to traverse our sharp edges. We slowly start to find that we're able to swim in waters that were at one time too treacherous. We begin teaching ourselves how to navigate these chilling streams without losing our way. As I navigated the waters of my memory, I practiced allowing myself to float, to stay buoyant and calm in the face of turbulent emotions. The good and the bad flowed together, ultimately revealing a much more cohesive picture of my father and of myself.

Remembrance will bring everything to the surface as soon as we declare that we're ready to take power over our lives. As we ask questions like *what can I do to resolve this pain*, it takes us out of victimhood and into conscious participation. We find ourselves becoming less resistant to looking at past frames of pain, no matter how they may resonate with us now. We get to interview these pains and ask *where did you come from? Why does this pain make me feel like I feel? How have I allowed this kind of pain to take over my life?* The way that we teach ourselves to navigate through these chilling streams without losing our way is to continue to cultivate courage through our willingness to look at the memories. We must convince ourselves to find a side of the pain or the memory that could possibly have a lesson to it.

As we further engage in self-inquiry, we might ask ourselves, *what did I learn from that experience back then? What can I learn from it now?* In this way we're retraining ourselves as we reframe our experiences. We now know that we don't always have to think back to the pain of a negative situation and immediately re-live the suffering it caused. Instead, we can ask ourselves, *how can that experience inform my growth and help me to live a greater life?* This isn't an easy task, but if we understand that there's another side to pain and disappointment, then the growing edge of our empowerment is choosing which side we want to live on.

Some of the memories that we encounter will be torturous and treacherous. We can look at where we are now and celebrate that we made it through those times. But how do we take this oil and water and make it so that emulsifies into something that can serve a greater purpose? The only way that oil and water mix is to have another compound or component that binds them together. Say the oil is the bad and the water is the good. The missing emulsifier is your participation, your willingness to take what has already happened and use it as fuel to continue on your path of self-discovery.

Perhaps the fact that your father was absent from your life has hindered your ability to connect with other people. However, you still realize that one day you'd like to be in a serious relationship and get married and have children. Certainly you'd never want your relationship with your spouse or your children to become like your relationship with your father. So, in some ways, what your father has given you is a roadmap to creating the type of relationship that you *do* want to have with your own children.

The more we do this work the more success we'll have on our healing path. This may even lead us to go back to our fathers and try to make amends, allowing them to see our own lives as demonstrations of what's possible. Hopefully they'll catch on to something that they can embrace in their own life. This is what happened between my dad and me. In the final years of his life, my father and I finally developed the kind of relationship that we both had silently yearned for throughout most of my life. When I let go of the anger and disappointment and sadness of the past, I was able to finally meet my father with unconditional love, which he eventually reciprocated in kind.

When we are unable to walk the path of healing, it can create a vicious generational cycle of anger, blame and shame. This is why many fathers leave the home. This is why many fathers are there but not actively present or emotionally available to their children. To break the cycle we have to bridge the old paradigms and the new paradigms. We're not necessarily talking about bridging ways of being. We're talking about bridging an understanding, which reminds us that there's something under the negative demonstrations that we've been subjected to. There's a history that has been passed down. When we get that, we can sit down and say, "Oh, that's the way it was. I understand now. I don't agree with it. I still don't like it, but at least I understand it."

That way, we start to release ourselves from becoming victim to that type of generational pathology. Now is the time for the cycles to be broken. But those cycles can only be broken as we give ourselves more opportunities to shift into change with knowledge and education.

Growth and transcendence doesn't happen overnight. Circumstances and events may still trigger old attitudes toward people. Things that are triggers in your life will remain triggers until you can come to an agreement with you self that the trigger isn't there to torment you. When you feel as though you're being tormented, the natural impulse is to run away. We want to do the exact opposite. We want to invite the memories in so we can initiate the process of acceptance and reframing.

One of the ways that we deal with triggers is to become cognizant of when we're becoming defensive. When someone says something and we automatically think that they're coming at us in an aggressive way, we become defensive. We put up walls of protection. There's something in the other person's comment that we believe is an attack on how we feel about ourselves. If we're not as confident in ourselves as we could be, we might feel the need to say something to make ourselves right. For myself when I become defensive I always have to "get you told." *Let me let you know this is how I feel!*

That type of behavior definitely comes from not being understood and not being heard. You don't have anyone to talk with you about your feelings. It's like you're forever walking around with a chip on your shoulder. Whatever someone says becomes a jab. You become so sensitive to your pain that you're like a walking wound. Everything and anything another person says can make you think that they're talking directly to you.

We must begin to become aware of any place where we become defensive and put up walls. Once we become aware, we have an invitation to become quiet. That's the time when not speaking is the best thing to do. If defensiveness is present, that means ego is running the show because it wants to be right. No matter how you try to phrase it, your words will come out defensive or angry because that's what happens when we're triggered. So the best thing to do is to be quiet and then talk to the part of you that's triggered or enraged.

When I speak to myself, I say things like, *wow why did that make me so mad?* I promise you the answer shall appear because you're hot enough for those types of insights to germinate. Seeds germinate when they are exposed to enough heat. Too much heat will destroy the seed and no heat at all will prolong the time that the seed takes to grow. But just the right amount of heat causes the life that is dormant within the seed to spring forth.

Journaling is another outlet, which will assist you in the process of self-inquiry. Sit and write about a moment when you felt triggered by something that someone else said or did, then step back and recognize how defensive, angry or anxious you actually became. This isn't about beating yourself up. It's about observation. Your observations help you become aware and watch what other types of things trigger you. Then you can continue to ask the question: *why do those things trigger me?*

So to recap, the ways in which we can use our power of remembrance to assist us on our healing journey are as follows: Step one is recognition. Step two is self-inquiry, which allows you to weed out that which no longer serves you. Step three is to replace the old reactions with new ways of responding. In other words we get to reframe our triggers. In the reframing process we find out how the memories really resonate with us. Do they continue to anger us even further? Do they take us spiraling down to even deeper levels of sadness and low self-esteem?

There's a big difference between unleashing on someone in a tirade of defensiveness and true empowerment. Most of the time when we act in defense it's a call or plea for someone to agree with us. *I'm pissed off at someone so I'm going to give him a piece of my mind!* And we normally look around for people to agree with what we've said, which gives more fuel to our tirade. But when we're confident in ourselves, we become settled rather than defensive. Our position may not be the popular or status quo opinion but we're settled in what we believe. There's no need to take someone else's viewpoint or dissent personally.

Our clarity and confidence has the ability to shift the contours of the conversation. Our viewpoint, our memories and our conversations invite something of an uplifting, eternal nature to come forth. So we've empowered ourselves to give back to those around us, rather than wallowing in anger or self-pity due to our past experiences. And what we receive is the fulfillment of having healthy conversations and healthy relationships with the people in our lives. And also with ourselves. Here, we agree to take the instructive path versus taking the destructive path.

Take a Breath

Set the intention that, when a person, memory or situation triggers you, rather than reacting in the old way stop and take a breath. Release the urge to become defensive and speak from the pain of the ego. Instead, sit back and allow yourself to become immersed in silence. Listen to what's going on within your soul rather than being part of a tirade of anger and defensiveness.

Questions and Answers

Write out some of the memories that have triggered sadness or painful disappointment or hatred within you.

We don't talk much about hatred in our society but sometimes that emotion resides underneath our socially acceptable interactions. Hate is taboo. But some men hate their fathers and they will tell you that. We want to bounce back quickly from those negative emotions. It takes a whole lot of energy for us to hate. When we live our lives from hate it's like feeding ourselves poison. We must unearth the feeling and acknowledge the pain and vulnerability behind it in order to neutralize and then release it.

_____
_____
_____
_____
_____
_____
_____
_____
_____
_____
_____
_____
_____
_____
_____
_____
_____
_____

_____

_____

_____

_____

_____

_____

_____

_____

_____

_____

_____

_____

_____

Power Three:
The Power of Self-Discovery

We all like to be affirmed and we'll go to great measures to make people think we're cool. The bottom line is that we want to be accepted. Human beings need connection, which is why it feels so painful to be ostracized. It often seems as though it will be easier to acquiesce to the status quo, what society says is normal, even if it means detaching from the truth of who we are. In my mind, I didn't know what was acceptable in my father's eyes, so I tried everything. Unfortunately, I never really succeeded at getting his acceptance.

At the base of the human experience is the desire for connection. Whether it's conveyed in the spoken word or felt deep in the heart, within almost any form of communication is the powerful need for connection. As we grow from childhood through adolescence, we're doing our best to navigate a world of discoveries. Everything is new and, for a while, everything seems possible. Our natural urge is to share our hopes, joys, dreams and discoveries with those closest to us. We want to connect with them, to be affirmed. Sons instinctively want to connect with their fathers and the blueprint that they believe the father has on life.

In short: Little boys want to be like their daddies.

A child yearns to experience connection with his father in many different ways, whether it's going out to play ball, having a basic conversation or just being in the same room as someone so loved and familiar. In healthy relationships, the experience of connection is important to both father and son. But when communication is cut off, the child's ability to learn by being around his father is stunted. The child is denied the connection and acceptance that is so crucial to his healthy development.

The kinds of thoughts that go through a child's mind when they have a close and meaningful relationship with their father might be something such as: *wow my daddy likes me. He likes spending time with me. My daddy is my friend. I like being around my father.* But when that doesn't happen the opposite occurs. The child feels rejected from that familiar face and body. It has heartbreaking effects on his thoughts about himself. One of the first things I thought when my father rejected me was: *wow there must be something wrong with me. It's obvious that he doesn't like being around me. He must think I'm strange.* If not corrected, these kinds of stories will build up in the child's mind.

Whether we realize it or not, after a while we've made an entire volume of assumptions. We can explain, in intimate detail, why we feel the way we feel about our fathers and why we don't like them and they don't like us. Even more damaging, that narrative also becomes a false narrative about ourselves.

As a child, it's hard to come back from that kind of thinking. Those beliefs and emotions move with you until you realize (usually well into adulthood) how the pain has tracked you throughout your life. Sometimes the only way to come back is to have the courage to recognize and acknowledge the pain of separation. Then, as we previously discussed, you can also acknowledge that you can do something about it. You might call and try to make things right with your father, even if you've never attempted something like that before. You could also seek counseling, either from a trained therapist or from others whom you respect who have been in similar situations.
Eventually it's going to become a job that you have to take on. And that means that you have to do some more work with self-counseling. Ask yourself questions like: *where did my issues with my father begin?* Then

work your way through that. You can take it a step further by saying to yourself: *This is who I have believed myself to be due to my father's actions. But now who do I say I am?*

Affirmations

Write out an affirmation where you describe in detail who you affirm yourself to be right now. For example: *I am a confident, abundant man of power. I live in integrity because I do what I say I'm going to do, when I say I'm going to do it. My promises have meaning.*

_____

_____

_____

_____

_____

_____

_____

_____

_____

_____

_____

When young men act out from the need to be acknowledged or affirmed, the results can be devastating. They have babies out of wedlock even when they aren't willing or able to take care of them. Some boys will go out and join gangs. Sometimes, to really rattle the nerves of mothers and grandmothers, who are the only supporting characters in their world, they'll stay away from home. They won't come back when they're supposed to, knowing that the women who love and care deeply for them are worrying about them all day and all night. They do this to get attention, to lash out at the only people available to them. When the man whose attention they're really trying to get isn't there to check them, they can step beyond as many boundaries as they want, because he can't do anything about it. He's not there.

We all know that children act out to get attention. But adults do the exact same thing as well. Acting out can be anything from yelling and screaming, to getting into trouble with the law, to not paying your bills on time. When we act out our pain and frustration rather than dealing with it head on, life becomes extremely volatile. When our behavior stems from the kind of unhealed emotional wounds that we've been discussing, what it really boils down to is a missed opportunity for connection between father and son.

The father is a keeper of order in the household. Little boys tend to view their relationship with their father as a safe haven. *If I've got a question about something important I can go ask my daddy. If I'm feeling weird or strange about myself I can go talk to my father. He won't judge me. He won't chastise me. We can sit down and have a conversation about it.* This is where the health of the communication is really important.

In some relationships the son might feel that he can go to his father, but may do so hesitantly. If the father's response is abrasive and harsh, then the son will say to himself: *I know I can go to daddy but he'll just tear me down and I don't want that right now. So I'm going to try to figure it out for myself.* He might not say it out loud but in his mind he's thinking that the only resolution is to go it alone.

When we're children and we don't receive the connection or guidance that we're seeking, anger and frustration mounts. We may feel confused or overwhelmed and our fathers aren't there to provide boundaries. It becomes easier to act up and rail against this invisible figure. If we're not careful and conscious this behavior can follow us into adulthood, coloring the kind of life we create.

We want our fathers to direct us; their presence helps us understand the need for healthy boundaries. We are looking for our fathers to tell us: *Yes, you will make missteps or mistakes but this is how you get back from the edge to the center, son.* So the child sees a huge pallet called life full of vibrant colors, but there aren't concrete signposts to instruct him on how far he can go. Mothers will do their best to enforce boundaries for their children. But after a while—particularly during adolescence when he's growing into manhood—the young man is desperately seeking an example that looks like him. When that example isn't there, he must flounder toward manhood without guidance. When a boy feels as though he has to learn to become man with no examples on how to do so, it becomes very scary.

When men seek to experience healthy forms of acknowledgment, affirmation and the need for boundaries, the healing process becomes paramount. The only way out is the journey in. The world is never going to tell you the truth of who you are. If you are going to find it, it's an inside journey. Seek out others who are on the same path. Attend men's groups or other gatherings that are centered on wholeness and healing. Support the men that you meet in these groups as they travel through the pains of their past on their own healing journey. This is a necessary step because if we don't know the origin of something we can only cure the symptoms. We can't cure the problem.

Sometimes the simplest things can help as we move through great transformation. Get out and exercise alone and with others. Play a game of basketball or football. We need to get far enough out of our habitual mindset so that we can breathe. And, if you're at the age of 30 or above, try to get out and play games with the young kids coming up behind you. They are able to teach us so many things about letting go. As you play ask yourself: *how is this game allowing me to release?*

We want to become conscious as we do these things. We want to become conscious of why we do what we do and how we talk to other people. Becoming conscious of who you really are and what your motivations are helps you to grow in self-acceptance.

Rather than acting out your aggressions, write it out in your journal and get some space between yourself and the action. See what you really want to experience as opposed to what emotions are pushing to get out in the moment. Writing takes some steam off. You may even want to write to your father and say something like:

Dear Dad, This is your son. I just wanted to let you know that I've been thinking about our relationship for a long time and how hard it's been. And I've been blaming you for the areas of my life that are a piece of crap. Be honest. What that does is gives us an opportunity to look back at our words and see where we're taking responsibility for our actions and where we're still living in judgment, hurt and blame. You get to see your true feelings on paper. They become a reflection of your innermost self, rather than having feelings that you project onto someone else.

We must begin to expose those places where we feel inadequate, or that we're not worth investing the time to become more active in our pathway towards wholeness. It's imperative to make the time to be with ourselves, and to be around things and people that exude self-worth and purpose. One of the simplest ways to do this is to get out into nature. Go for a walk. Sit down in the middle of a garden. Be with those things that have no ulterior motive. They aren't trying to outdo or outrun anything. They are stationary in their purpose and they are fine with what they are. There are many things we could learn from taking a few minutes to meditate on our relationship with nature.

Most men on some level feel that there's great danger in exposing their inadequacies or vulnerabilities. Strength is looked at as being a prime quality for a man, which is integral to self-worth and self-confidence. In fact, it's supposed to be a hallmark of manhood. However, being able to acknowledge your vulnerabilities to yourself is actually a great strength that we would do well to cultivate. It means that you're now taking full responsibility for the things you do and say, and how you go about your life. Part of being vulnerable is admitting to things that you've always known about yourself that you've been afraid to address outside your own mind. But not addressing the areas where you need to stretch and grow keeps you from experiencing the fullness of your self-worth and self-esteem.

Vulnerability is a great trait to have when you sit down and talk about things that make you feel sad or hurt or angry. Being able to see yourself clearly and accept yourself fully is the true essence of strength. Strength is not about being right all the time. It's not about sexual or physical prowess. It's not about who's smarter or who's right or wrong. It's about being honest with yourself. When you're not honest you run the risk of perpetuating miscommunication, half-truths, and outright lies. When you do that you also perpetuate the vicious cycles that have created these painful experiences from generation to generation.

Releasing negative consciousness really boils down to having the courage to reconnect with your authentic self. One of my favorite ways of reconnecting with myself is to go out alone in nature, as I mentioned before. We can take this even a step further by taking ourselves on retreat. Take a retreat from your family. You might even want to take a retreat from your job. If you're single, it's a great opportunity to be by yourself. Sometimes we think we need to be with someone else most (if not all) of the time. If that's true of you, ask yourselves the question: *why do I feel like I need to have somebody with me? Am I afraid to be alone?*

Conversely, there're many people who isolate themselves, particularly when going through troubling times. If you're one of those people, perhaps you should ask yourself: *why do I try to avoid connection? Am I afraid of being abandoned or let down again? How can I begin to embrace others?*

Some of these are very hard questions. They often boil down to one central point: why have I chosen to live my life the way that I'm living it? Asking that question will bring up a whole lot of things, both good and bad. Until we become conscious, we'll find that much of the way we have chosen to live our lives is in reaction to the choices made by absentee fathers. We must learn to recognize what thoughts and decisions were his as opposed to the thoughts and decisions and beliefs are actually belong to us. That leads us to ask the question: *what have I believed about what people have said about me versus what I say about my self? Is this the job I really want? Is this the right relationship for me? Am I living my life or am I living the life of someone else?*

Take a Breath

Find your favorite picture. Look at the picture or see it in your mind's eye. Ask yourself what the photographer or artist was thinking about when he or she constructed this picture? What was the initial intent for the beneficial quality of the picture?

_____

_____

_____

_____

_____

_____

_____

_____

_____

Questions and Answers

Name three things that you are beginning to discover about the true essence of who you are.

_____

_____

_____

_____

_____

_____

_____

Power Four:
The Power of Compassion

When we deny our compassion, choosing instead to blame others for our experiences, we cut off our ability to transcend our circumstances. Blame is where we've chosen to believe something about what someone else did to us, or what we did to ourselves, to the extent that we're no longer willing to look at how our consciousness can be shifted. Blame is a victim's tool. When we want a scapegoat for what we think is wrong with us, we blame someone else for the way that we turned out.

When we choose blame over compassion, we give away our power to the very people we believe hurt us the most. We allow them to run our lives in the sense that their actions are the catalyst that determines our emotional state. Choosing to offer compassion rather than blame to those who have wronged us shifts that dynamic. Compassion isn't letting anyone off the hook. It's choosing to look at our situation from a much broader perspective. And the most powerful form of compassion is self-compassion. Practicing self-compassion means coming to terms with the fact that we do make mistakes, sometimes big ones, and that it's OK. We make a concerted effort to be easier with ourselves and not judge what we've done.

Instead, we use those missteps as steppingstones to becoming more aware of the patterns and behaviors of the past so that we won't repeat them again. As we learn to have more compassion for ourselves, we can then apply the same principles and processes when it comes to other people. But when we say, *I'm not going to let go. I won't release or forgive them for what they've done,* what we're really saying is I *'m going to allow what they said and did to hold sway over how I live my life.*

Most of time, this is done unconsciously. When we see the guilty person again, we immediately jump to a whole different mind frame— one of anger or hurt or resentment. But living with blame is like living in a puppet master's dream. You become a puppet, allowing someone else to pull your strings and run your life. The first step to releasing blame is to candidly acknowledge that we have been manipulated in the past and that we're living in a state of shame and blame in relation to those people and/or situations.

These are hard things to admit. People don't like to talk about shame. But everyone experiences shame at some time or another. Shame and blame are like twins. Both emotions cause us to live in a depleted, powerless state of mind. When we're living in shame we form thoughts such as *I'm not good enough. I didn't live up to what they said. I feel ashamed because it didn't work out like it was supposed to.* If we don't do the inner work to root out all of the ways that we've held onto the shame, we'll even harbor the thought *I'm like this because of him.*

To release these unhealthy patterns, we must admit to ourselves the times that we don't feel good about ourselves. We must acknowledge that we've believed ourselves to be less than. We must tell the truth about all the ways that we've allowed what someone else has said about us to deflate us. There has to be conscious recognition of where we are now in order to move from blame to buoyancy. The next step is to pinpoint the holes in our psyche where we see the face of shame popping through, and then ask: *Where did that belief come from? Where did it originate? When did I start blaming someone else for the way that I felt?* We can also ask ourselves: *what am I going to do to counter those thoughts?*

This is about establishing the habit or practice of creating a new mental script. It can feel very scary to acknowledge someone who hasn't been present for you—and who may never show any intention of being present. It's an understandable defense mechanism for the ego to say: *I don't need him anyway.* It's difficult to let that go and acknowledge the impact of missing something so fundamental. The beginning of the excavation process, where you become more in tune with your self-compassion, is to first look squarely at your hurt.

That's not to say that we wallow in the pain. But we do sit with our need for our father's loving presence and his guidance. It may be as simple as saying to yourself, *I acknowledge that it would have been great to have him around.* For others, the process may be fraught with emotions, from numbness to betrayal to rage. Some of us have never even seen our fathers. We may not know if the man is alive or dead. In this case, we may be on a quest to finally see him so that we can put a face to our thoughts and feelings. No matter what the situation looks like, acknowledging helps you flip the script and take hold of your power.

Create Your Own Script

Ask yourself this question: *what would my life have been like if I had written the script of my father-son relationship, rather than him writing a script of abandonment?* Visualize and feel how you would've liked it to be. Allow your emotions and vulnerability to speak. (Remember, write as much as you want here and feel free to use more space in another journal to complete the exercise.)

_____

_____

_____

_____

_____

_____

_____

_____

As you do this exercise, you're actually creating a blueprint on how you'd want your relationship to be with your own sons and daughters. You can even use this exercise to reinvent how you'd like your relationship to be with your self. We're using this process to re-parent ourselves in loving, committed and healthy new ways. Another word for re-parenting is *reframing*. Who's the parent? The parent becomes a whole new consciousness.

Part of developing the compassion that can change your life is mustering up the courage to acknowledge the fact that the father figure is one of the most important figures in your life experience. Rather than trying to deny the importance of his presence, recognize your primal, basic need to connect with your father and allow the accompanying emotions to come forth.

There are many things that happen when you acknowledge a deeply held belief, versus downplaying it or ignoring it. The most important is the internal shift that makes resolution suddenly possible. Many people prefer to say, *I did just fine by myself. I'm glad he wasn't there.* But what if a father figure had been present? How different would it be? Not acknowledging a loss is still sitting in the pain of it.

We blame our fathers for not being there and then we cut off our emotions by saying, *good I'm glad he wasn't there anyway.* But blame— whether we're blaming our fathers or ourselves—takes us away from being able to own the decisions that we've made in our lives. Acceptance and acknowledgment allows us to say, *I did my best. Would it have been great if my dad had been here with me? Yes. But I can't hold him to it. In the process I'm going to be better to myself. I'm going to be kinder to myself. I'm going to take better care of my self physically, emotionally, spiritually, and in every other way.* When you start to cultivate that type of compassion, it softens those hard places that you've been treading on for years. There will never be any real progress in your healing until compassion begins to grow.

Meditation is essential to this part of the process. If we don't regularly take time to get still, we'll find busy things to keep our minds off of the painful stuff. We find habits to keep us numb to the realization of what's really affecting us. Sit and be still. Then, when the emotions arise, let them come. Feel them fully. *I feel like my father deserted me. It does matter. It hurts.* Allow those feelings to surface and give them a way to be released. Let yourself cry. Let yourself be overcome by the emotions. Let the pain touch you so much that you release through tears if necessary.

That's a brave thing to do because men are taught not to cry and not to show how we really feel. Start listening to your words to determine whether they reflect the true depth of your feelings. If we want to own our integrity, then we need to listen to what we're saying. Because somewhere inside when we say we're doing great and we're really not, we have to then find a way to justify what we just said. That's when social codes and cultural branding begins to uphold us, rather than our truth.

Start listening to the inner talk, your inner voice, instead of what has transpired in the past. Rather than turning the volume up on your cell phone and all of that, turn up the volume on your inner voice. Get somewhere where you can be quiet. Get away from the chatter. Listen. Do whatever it takes to get you in a meditative state. If it's running on the treadmill for an hour where you can think, do it.

Healing the pain that has hampered our mental development can also heal the pain that lingers in the body. If we believe in the oneness of the physical, mental, emotional and spiritual bodies, then it would make sense that they can help one another along the path toward healing and growth. Progress in one area can lead to progress in others. In other words, if you're going through something that's causing you to feel sad or bad, get up and start walking.

So, again, the first step is to sit down and get quiet. Being in silence develops and fine-tunes the process of hearing what's going on within, rather than being distracted by what's going on all around us. When we get quiet we can pick up on our inner conversation, which we've been calling self-inquiry or self-counsel thus far. This is a critical skill that we must master.

Compassion is a spiritual quality that holds within it a vortex of energy. The most powerful point of compassion is the self. When we are able to have compassion for our own missteps and shortcomings, we're able to be more loving and generous toward others. When people are willing to look through your mistakes and missteps (because most of us know when we've taken a misstep or when we've crossed the lines of disrespect) when compassion is shown to us in those moments, it does something to the mind and heart. It allows us to release the angst around what we know that we've done. Through that release, it becomes possible to engage a whole new point of view and a whole new way of being without the baggage of shame or guilt. In that instant, we are able to say, "I want to do better. I want to be better."

Most of the time we want to get it right and we have in our minds that there's a single path to getting it right. But our ideas about getting it right are often full of thoughts about what we did wrong. So even when we think we've finally gotten it right, we somehow fall back into the thought that it's just not good enough. We fall prey to beating ourselves up. Even when we've worked ourselves ragged we can still be bombarded by thoughts of *it's not good enough*. When that happens, we're not even able to see what we've accomplished.

We're always chasing something, trying to be better, trying to be enough. The chase can look many different ways. But the common denominator is that we go on autopilot and stop seeing what's really in front of us. But if we dare to go deep below the surface, we'd understand that it's not that we're not good enough for ourselves. Somewhere along the line we've conjured up a belief that says we're not good enough for somebody else—specifically our fathers. So we try and accumulate things, seeking to somehow appease him or outdo him. Or else we may start to act just like him. Either way, it becomes a downward spiral of judgment and recrimination. It's impossible for self-compassion to exist in that kind of hostile mental environment.

When we need help developing compassion for ourselves, one way to begin is by treating ourselves well, even—and especially—if we don't feel that we deserve it. Practice treating yourself the way you retreat someone you love deeply. Perhaps you provide yourself with some time off to pamper yourself. Take yourself on vacation. Get away from the business for a little while. Maybe you've always wanted to learn a foreign language. Do it. Or make it a point to meet five new people that you wouldn't otherwise engage. Try going to a restaurant and eating food that you normally wouldn't eat. Trying different things gets us out of our comfort zone.

As we get out and experience other things and other people, ask yourself: *what do I think about these things? What do I think about Spanish? Maybe I'd rather try French but either way I'm going to try something different.* Get out of your present environment and get yourself into places that may not be so familiar. This gives you the opportunity to take a breath and get your mind off of your tirades, which may have been going on for years.

Take a Breath

Let's do a meditation on thankfulness here. Be thankful for whatever it is that you have, even if you may feel that it's not enough. Be thankful and say it: *I am thankful for what I have. I am grateful for my life. I'm willing to live a better life. I'm willing to be compassionate towards myself and towards others. I'm willing to release the past.*

The Peace Poem

We're going to write a poem here as a means of expressing ourselves. This may not feel familiar or comfortable but that's all right.

Your poem doesn't have to rhyme. It just needs to have deep meaning for you. This is called a Peace Poem.

Write a poem about your life. What do you really feel about your life? Whatever we write, at the end of the poem we're going to make peace with it. This is the next step in the process that we began with the *I am willing* meditation. Now, we're saying, *I am willing to look at my life. I am willing to change. I'm willing to open up. But first, I must make peace with what is.*

When we make peace with what is, we give ourselves permission to move into what's possible.

_____
_____
_____
_____
_____
_____
_____
_____
_____
_____
_____
_____
_____
_____
_____
_____

Affirmation

Find one area of your life in which you know you can do better. Write an affirmation in the present tense stating how you are stepping into a new way of being in this area. (I Am a loving and responsible father to my children. I Am physically, emotional and financially present in their lives at all times. I've learned from the missteps and the pains of my past and commit to doing better and being better everyday.)

_____

_____

_____

_____

_____

_____

_____

_____

Questions and Answers

Come up with three ways that you're going to treat yourself better from now on. For each of those ways, write out in detail how you're going to do it. What is your participation in allowing a new way of being to unfold?

_____

_____

_____

_____

_____

_____

_____

_____

_____

_____

Power Five: **The Power of Surrender**

There are layers and layers and layers in the letting go process, just like there are layers and layers in the forgiveness process. The important part of the process of letting go is that we take the initial jump. In pertaining to the relationship with our fathers, we are being given the opportunity to reconcile the negative thoughts that we may have harbored. We get to remove our fathers from the mental prison that we've held them in, perhaps for years. We're now willing, in our minds and deep in our hearts, to dig under years and layers of mental garbage to find the key that will release them.

The process of letting go is so deep, multilayered and challenging mainly because we've gone through our whole lives taking the raw materials of our experience and adding our subjective beliefs to the mix. Our experiences take on a life and history of their own, so that they become living things to us. For example, when I was small I would ask my father, "Daddy, will you come out and play with me?" He'd reply, "No I've got to go do a job." But that was just the beginning because I'd take his response to mean something totally different. I put layers of meaning on top of the situation.

I'd make an entire monologue in my mind to support my conclusion:

My daddy said he doesn't want to play ball with me because he doesn't like me. He doesn't want to be around me. He probably thinks that I don't play as well as my brother. When we continue to give life to the pain that we've experienced, it becomes a deeper-seated pain. Eventually, we'll start to live our lives through the prism of the pain. Sometimes we do this knowingly, but most of the time we do it unknowingly. We make life-changing decisions not based on the options that are in front of us, but based on our old pain. We get in and out of relationships based on pain.

So the process of releasing and letting go isn't just a one-time process. It's not just something that you can wake up one day and say *I'm free of this pain.* Pain has many faces to it and it has ways of creeping into every area of life. In order to work through the layers on our way to freedom, we again come to the process of self-counseling. Do you want to find the emotional root of where the pain started? When a thought triggers you, ask yourself: *why do I keep going in circles with this thought? It's ruining my life and driving me crazy. Where did it come from? Where did it begin?* The answer will show itself to you if you're willing to get quiet, listen and dissect the response that arises, rather than running from it and thinking that you're crazy.

This is the first and most important step: understanding that your perception of pain had a genesis, a beginning. Consciously recognizing the root of our pain allows us to stop pretending that life has the power to randomly trigger us and that we can just blow up at any time for any reason. No, the question is: *why do I blow up and when did I start doing that? What makes me really angry?* These are the series of questions that we must ask ourselves if we ever want to be free. Another important question is: *do I want to continue to be angry (or sad or frustrated or jealous)? Am I willing to continue to live my life this way?* The pain will surely continue to run us if we let it. It will guide us and steer us in every direction possible. But that's not a fulfilling journey.

Healing is a process. It's not something done overnight. We take the huge step of beginning the process because we want to form stronger relationships. We want to be more bonded with our self-esteem. We want to understand our self-worth. That's what we're really talking about—our relationship with ourselves. Even if we started this journey trying to heal relationships with other people in our lives, the truth is that we can't make someone else come along on the journey with us. We can do what we do and participate the best way that we can, but we can't make other people adhere to the healing path in the ways that we think they should. This is part of the process of releasing our fathers from the mental prisons in which we've held them for so long.

Completing these steps requires courage, particularly our work in releasing our fathers. You may decide to call your father and acknowledge to him how you feel about him. That takes courage. You could say something like, *Dad I'm glad you were part of my being born.* Even if that's the only positive thing that you can find to say to your father, the success lies in your willingness and ability to say it.

Can you think of three ways in which your father has played a definitive role in your ability to be here, where you are, on the planet at this time? Of course, he sired you. That's the obvious first answer. Without that you wouldn't be here. But what else has he contributed to you? Somewhere in that answer is the possibility that he loves you. There's also the possibility that he, too, wants to heal. Just keeping these things in mind (whether you actually make a call and find answers to these questions or not) takes your father out of the realm of being a villain in your life story. It brings him into the realm of being human, which helps in the releasing process. When we humanize our fathers it aids us in our quest to have compassion for them, rather than just distain or even hatred.

Exercise

We want to humanize our vision of our fathers. To that end, write out the answer to this question: *how was my father's relationship with his father?*

_____

_____

_____

_____

_____

_____

_____

_____

_____

_____

_____

It doesn't matter what answers you came up with, as long as you answered to the best of your ability with whatever knowledge you have. This is the question that broke the ice for me in terms of my understanding of my father and his emotional landscape. You may find that your father's relationship with his father was much like your relationships with him. If this is true, it indicates a number of things.

Number one, there's intergenerational pain involved. Ask yourself if you want this intergenerational disturbance of communication to continue? Do you want your relationship with your children, particularly with your sons if we have them, to be like your relationship with your father, and his with his father? We must think deeply about how we break cycles. Here is another question to consider: *Is this cycle part of my authentic self? Is this the reason why certain things are so painful to me?*

If your father is deceased or you have no way of contacting him, you can still do a variation of this exercise. Ask yourself: *what would my relationship with my father look like if he were not dead/absent? If I had to create my own relationship with my father what would it have been like?* Write out your answer below.

_____

_____

_____

_____

_____

Awakening is closely aligned with change and transformation. It's like trying on a new mental suit. It also has to do with shedding. When we commit to the process of shedding (or surrendering) old ideas and perceptions, we give ourselves more room to fit into the new energy that's unfolding around us in our lives. Otherwise, we continue to live in a space that we've outgrown. That causes constriction on every area of our lives to the point where we literally feel like we cannot breathe. Refusing to let go of what no longer serves us keeps us from becoming conscious. There's no room to grow.

Awakening is becoming conscious, becoming aware. The questions that we just posed at the end of the last section can get us to the point where we wake up to a more compassionate vantage point. I'd always held my father in the strict confines of his role as "dad." Only much later did I come to the conscious realization that he was a human, a man with a past just like myself, who also carried deep hurt. That realization began to change my entire outlook. It also got me to the point where I was willing to surrender my hardness toward him.

Learning about the humanity of my dad opened up the possibility that his experiences could be parallel to my experiences, which makes me human with him. I began to glimpse sides of my father I'd never known. When we overturn our emotional soil, it allows us to plant new seeds. Before I came to these realizations, my father was always tucked away in the back of my mind because I was always playing the role of victim. That ended when I finally came to recognize that neither of us was inferior or superior to the other. We were both human and if we had the same pains, hurts and successes, it was also possible that we could heal together.

As we awaken, we're actually inviting a whole litany of new thoughts and beliefs to come to the table of possibility where we're learning new ways of processing our experiences. After a while we can't think the same old thoughts. We have new information that has changed our outlook. Anytime there's an old paradigm and the new paradigm existing in the same place at the same time, there has to be an integration period to allow what no longer serves us to be released. We take a leap of faith and put ourselves in new situations where we're pulled by a new vision and new awareness.

When I first made the choice to forgive my dad, the exercise that I gave myself was this: *the next time you call mom, ask to speak to him. Every time you call home from now on when you're ending your conversation with your mother, ask to speak to him and tell him that you love him. See what he says.* That was my way of taking on courage and asking courage to be my friend. Because I knew that if my father did not respond (and he didn't for a very long time) it would be devastating. But that's when you have the opportunity to couple your new awakening with integrity and intention. Integrity and intention are the spiritual qualities, which say, *no matter what the outcome I'm going to stick to what I know. And I know that I love my daddy. I know that if it hadn't been for my father I wouldn't be here. That is the truth.*

Surrendering the elements of our past that are holding us back is an ongoing life process. Self-discovery is a lifelong beautiful journey. And in the course of that journey, we're able to see things that we've never seen before. Surrender allows us to become clear on how to move through the seeming chaos and emotional upheaval that comes into everyone's life experience at some point. As we breathe, we find that we're able to let go easily and gracefully. You can't bring the old thoughts and beliefs with you as you cross over into new understanding. Something has to give. You can't bring the old patterns with you, because you've crossed over into a whole different realm of thought. But you must bring them up, remember them and honor them fully, in order for them to be neutralized.

As we become more adept at the art of surrender, there's less intention and concentration on forcing a specific outcome. We're more focused on the present moment. For example, when I called my father, I released the urge to rush through the conversation to see whether he would respond to my *I love you.* Instead, I focused on being present in the conversation and learning more about who he was and being vulnerable enough to share my authentic self with him. So surrender is about letting the expectations go. That's when it becomes really good because we find ourselves engaged in honest self-discovery.

When I think of surrender I think of the energy that courses through me when I sing. When I was on Broadway I used to manipulate the notes I sang at auditions because I wanted the job. So I used to say to myself, *right here I'm going to hit that high note. Then I'm going to go down into my mid-range and then I'll take it back up. And that'll get me the job.* On and on and on. But after a while I started not getting the job and so I thought, *there's someplace else that I can embellish.* But at the end of the day, what I found out was that singing is telling a story in a song. If I did that without trying to get to the end or trying to get a job, then I'd have enjoyed all of the in-between time from walking in the door to walking out.

It's like that with any relationship but particularly the father-son relationship. The last three or four years of my father's life I wasn't trying to get anything from him. I had told him I loved him for years and years before he finally said it back. I didn't tell him I love him to hear him say it back. That wasn't the intention. The intention of the conversation was about finding out more about the human side of my father. So I had to surrender my outcome and my expectations. What I received in return far outweighed anything I could have orchestrated, including my own hard-won lessons in self-discovery.

The chaos and emotional upheaval that comes through everyone's life experiences at some point are rooted in our expectations. We create ideas around what we expect someone else to say and what we want him or her to do—the end result. And if that means changing who we are, changing the way we talk, changing the way we dress, trying to curry favor just to get what we want from them, life becomes chaotic. Not only that, after a while that doesn't work. We start to run out of ways of manipulating situations and people. Life is much simpler, and more fulfilling, when we allow ourselves to surrender to the moment and honor the truth that lies within it.

Take a Breath

As we move from one paradigm, or thought process, to another we must leave room for a period of integration to take place. That process can feel very overwhelming and the best thing to do is to breathe through it. Then make a concerted effort to break yourself out of the old mold. If and when you decide to speak with your father about this journey, make sure to do something affirming for yourself afterward. Take a long walk, so that you can give the new information a way and a place to process through you. Keep any new information you receive to yourself at first. Allow it to speak to you in ways that you understand. One of the most powerful things you can do is to hold your new insights and possibilities in sacred silence. Because the relationship that you're building with your father, and with your self, is sacred.

Questions and Answers

Ask yourself this question: *what would a healthy relationship with your father (or with the memory of your father) look like to you?*

———————————————————————————————
———————————————————————————————
———————————————————————————————
———————————————————————————————
———————————————————————————————
———————————————————————————————
———————————————————————————————
———————————————————————————————
———————————————————————————————
———————————————————

Color Your Life

For this exercise, I want you to get a large piece of paper and a box of crayons or colored pens or markers. Draw a line, or continuum, on the page. Fill in the spaces on this continuum with different colors, which represent the different phases of experience with your father.

Start from the youngest age that you can remember and begin to color your relationship with your father from the thoughts that spring to mind. These pictures can be abstract swirls of light and dark colors or they can be actual images that represent certain times and situations that stand out in your mind. Notice any color changes or patterns that begin to emerge. When and where do the colors change? Did you reach a certain age where the "colors" of your relationship shifted? Was there a specific event or series of events that caused this change?

If I had colored my relationship with my father, for example, it would've gone from some bright streaks during my early years to darker hues as I approached eight years old. Then it would've gone to very dark colors as I approached adolescence. Now, let's take mental snapshots of the continuum and think about how these time periods relate to different parts of your life. We get to dissect the areas where the colors are differentiated and walk through what the colors represent in terms of our emotional states and events of childhood.

Affirmation

Say this out loud to yourself: *I am more than capable of peeling back layers of pain and disappointment. I surrender my ideas of how things should have been, and I choose to embrace my freedom.*

Power Six:
The Power of Authentic Integrity

The greatness that we were all born to manifest can be activated by the conscious development of our character. There's a huge distinction between personality and character, though many people don't understand the difference. Personality can be swayed heavily by social coding, rather than our indwelling spiritual coding. It is often influenced by external expectations that have informed us on how we think we should act. Character, on the other hand, has to do with allowing ourselves to uncover the deep secrets of the inner voice that's always speaking. When individuals become snared in the cult of personality that's so prevalent in our culture, they waste their time trying to create these vast, spectacular, magnetic personalities so that people will like them and so that they'll feel better about themselves. But character is the real filter that leads us into our own brilliance. So, whatever we come to understand about the authentic essence of who we are will not be shaken or confined by the limitations of our personality. We're not defined by our personality.

Try to imagine people throwing clothes into a big heap. The pile has clothes of all sizes and colors and styles. See yourself rummaging through the heap, checking out every shirt and pair of pants that you think you like. You try some on before realizing that they don't fit. It may take a while—a long while—before you find something that is just right for you.

This is what the process of growing up is like. We try out all sorts of styles and personas, trying to "find ourselves." Our families, friends and society in general throw a lot of ideas at us in terms of who we should be and how we should act. What types of manners should we have? Everyone has an opinion. Now, of course, having good manners is important. But sometimes manners, like other facets of our behavior, can be imposed on us because of certain social or cultural codes that hold sway in a particular time or place. Manners and social codes have even passed down from generation to generation, from father to son, as survival tactics. But inevitably customs change or fade away. Our families and friends may all have different ideas about who we should be. We're left wondering, *should I act according to the social status quo? Or do I need to follow my own rules and act according to what feels responsible to me?*

What separates a man's character from his personality is personal responsibility. We become truthful when we take on character. We become what people want us to be when we settle into personality traits. Character speaks to our personal integrity. We don't just say things that we think will make us look fantastic and cool. We invite stability into our experience when we build character.

Men who leave their families without making emotional and financial provision for their children show a lack of character; they don't have the ability to be honest with themselves. If you can't be honest with yourself, you can't be honest with your spouse. If you can't be honest with your spouse, you can't be honest with your children. Life becomes unstable as you try to maneuver around things instead of standing in your power. Blame and shame also come with being unstable because the victim consciousness is always trying to highlight fault in someone else, rather than focusing on becoming centered within self.

Many of us missed out on the character building lessons that we imagine we would've had if our fathers had been present. If this is the case, we must be even more vigilant about cultivating our relationships with our own children or other young people that need our guidance. Make it a point to spend quality time passing down these character-building ideas. The time spent together is important because that's when communication happens. Communication is a powerful tool. In our family life, we get to access the truth of who we are by listening to someone else's opinion and then asking: *is that what I truly believe? Is that what I'd like to practice in my life?*

We can consider our family our own personal recreation center because everybody is a different ballgame. Your parents and siblings create different fields for you to play on. You get to find the field that you want to play on and begin to honor your own rules. This brings us back to character. When we haven't had a positive male role model to showcase strong character and integrity, we must develop our own tools to help build our own character. We must learn for ourselves why embracing responsibility is a good thing rather than something to run from.

There are some tools that can help with this process. First, find yourself a mentor. Your mentor can be an individual that you know personally or even someone you've never met. When I played football growing up, I felt a kinship with the football player Charles White who played for the University of Southern California. I considered him my mentor because I wanted to be a great football player just like him. I watched him on his journey to becoming a Heisman Trophy winner and paid close attention to his Heisman speech, in which he gave thanks to his family and his team. This indicated to me that he knew he was part of something larger than himself. That was the type of person I wanted to be. I'd never met Charles White. But I didn't need to in order to recognize the traits of strength, honor and integrity that I wanted to emulate.

So, one path to finding a mentor is to devote yourself to something that you love to do and then find someone you really look up to who's doing the same thing. It could be someone in your neighborhood—maybe an older guy that you respect or one of your colleagues. Look at the qualities of your mentor and use them as a template to start developing your own characteristics. Another great mentor of mine was the singer Donny Hathaway. I loved the way Donny Hathaway sang. But the real character that was evident to me within his music was the way that Donny Hathaway could tell a brilliant story while singing the song. That was important to me. It made me want to touch others with my musical gifts the way that Donny Hathaway touched my life.

When you don't have a father figure, having a strong male presence that provides you with guidance and inspiration can be a powerful key to finding strength within yourself. However, though mentors are important they can never replace your father. Eventually we will still have to take this journey to heal the father-son relationship. It's inevitable. When we don't heal the relationship the pain of it will resurface. It has to because pain always has to be dealt with somewhere down the line before it can be resolved.

The world will never, ever give us a true perspective on who we are. It will always feed circumstance, conditions, situations and the past into the equation. As we commit to really understanding the character of our being, we are given the opportunity to embrace the fact that we're part of a whole. Thoughts of loneliness, fatherlessness and abandonment have one thing in common. They all put us into the action of separation. We may even want to be alone after a while because we think no one understands us. We're victims. We believe that we've been ostracized from the entire world based on how we feel about what one person says about us. In the process of becoming reinstated into a global social community, we have to come to some agreement that we do belong.

And if I don't think I belong, I'm going to try to fit in one more time.

As children, our fathers represent home to us. Even if the father isn't present there's still a longing in every child for a male figure who embodies that sense of belonging. Children know energies. I believe that children know the importance of balancing energies within the home. Being an initial relationship, the relationship with the father often dictates how a young man will feel about himself. Many young men secretly believe that if this representative of manhood has rejected them, then they'll inevitably face rejection again and again as they make their way through society.

The father represents so much to the young mind. He's like the world. When the questions that a child has for his father aren't addressed, the child feels that there's no outlet for him to express his concerns. Missing out on the very simple things can create an almost cosmic catastrophe in the mind of a child or young man. That's when many become reclusive. But the reclusiveness is just a short-lived phase before the acting out begins. The sense of separation brings constriction; the feeling of loss is literally squeezing the life out of you and there appears to be no outlet for the expression of that energy.

This isn't an easy road to travel but it happens quite often. Young men who feel that they've been ostracized are often so magnetic that they attract other young men who feel the same way—that they've been separated from society. These young men sometimes form groups (or gangs) because the history of pain that they live with becomes synergized around the need to relate to other young men who understand. Sometimes they inflict pain on other people, which is really an indication of how they feel about themselves. They live from pain to pain.

But there are many things that we can do to foster feelings of community and to help us make the agreement within ourselves that we do belong. For fathers who are present in their own households but still struggling with the pains of their unhealed wounds, take your son or nephew to hang around the men that you hang around. Take him to the barbershop. Take him to church. Get him out into the larger community where there are other men who are present and interacting with him.

The male energy of communion is a very specific energy. It can be enhanced if we, as men, take note of women. Watch how they can sit down after a long day's work and have a good old talk. That connection takes away a whole lot of the stress and pain that men continue to wallow in because they keep it bottled inside. We don't feel like we can talk to anyone. We want to somehow get better all by ourselves. The truth is that we can start the process of healing alone, but at some point we're going to have to communicate with others as an outlet.

For the young men who are struggling with fatherlessness, I strongly urge you to journal about your experience. I cannot express the importance of this enough. The process takes what you're feeling and gets it out into another space besides your own mind. Once you write it, read it. Don't just write it and store it away in a drawer somewhere. Read your words. Keep your words handy so you can come back to them in a few days to read it again. If you feel that you need to make adjustments to what you've written, do it. Come back two or three weeks later and read it again so that your feelings have someplace beside your mind and your body to rest.

Exercise

Designate a certain period of the day to journal. No television, no texting and no e-mailing. Start with five minutes of dedicated writing time each day. We're talking about uplifting ourselves so that we can uplift others.

If the patterns of our childhoods are never fully healed, we'll continue to act out these unresolved disappointments and wounds no matter what our age. When you don't graduate, your life eventually begins to unravel. As men, we must step up and demand better from ourselves and from each other. Excellence is about doing your best at all times. Integrity is about keeping your word no matter what. Equanimity is the grounds for self-respect, so that you can learn to respect others. When core principles like these are taught, passed down from father to son, man to man, we see the fruits of our labor manifest in, through, and as us, as we become a beneficial presence wherever we are. On the other hand, if we choose to bypass them, we leap into personality-driven tricks that cast nets on a life filled with a desperate hope and one that stands on unstable ground.

Graduation is a term that I use for waking up and becoming conscious to greater degrees. We want to continue to evolve consciously and not get stuck in how things were or how we used to think or how we believe we can still manage. We begin to see things differently. We recognize that cultivating a quality like excellence is not like trying to get a destination. Excellence isn't a place; it's a way of life. What excellence does is continue to get us to ask the question: *am I my doing my best?* If you pass 10th grade geometry with flying colors, you're not going to get through 11th grade trigonometry believing that the same effort you used to pass geometry is the same effort needed for trigonometry. You know why? Because they're two totally different types of math. So there's an awareness that you've stepped into a different environment.

When you're still stuck in on a path that's twelve steps behind where you need to be now, it creates a conflict. That's when we try to play tricks and make up games. Most of them are blame games, which are centered in not taking responsibility. Awareness and responsibility can be difficult qualities to take on when there hasn't been a father figure around to demonstrate them. If that demonstration hasn't been apparent, when you get in a crunch you'll try to back out of your assignment. You'll try to get by doing less. But that doesn't work.

Responsibility and integrity require us to be committed to ourselves first. A young man who is committed to being true to his word can then be committed to the homework. He can be committed to his basketball team. He can be committed to coming home and doing the chores he's been asked to do. Young men who understand commitment, responsibility and integrity grow into adult men who are able to stand as examples and leaders.

Responsibility creates a snowball effect of momentum. It creates courage. We create a world where we think about intentions. That's where order comes in. When we don't have a demonstration of the male presence creating and maintaining order in a household, we have to create it for ourselves. That way somebody else coming behind us can see the demonstration. Our efforts create a spiral effect upward. Then we can stand in our priorities and say, *my life is important. How I live is important not just to me, but to people around me.*

Take a Breath

Take a breath and say to yourself, *I can commit to me. I can commit to my good. That's what's important to me right now. I can begin to build the legacy called me.*

Questions and Answers

Answer this question in the space below: *What does the legacy called you look like?*

_____
_____
_____
_____
_____
_____
_____
_____
_____
_____
_____

Project: Create Your Life

Find a chalkboard or a large piece of paper and a pencil. Begin to write down the things that are in your life right now. Your list might include headings like your girlfriend/wife, your children, your job, your hobbies, etc. If you're wearing your blue and green sneakers that represent the Seattle Seahawks and those are important to you, write that down too. Now look at your board.

Ask yourself the question: *are there things written on this board that no longer serve me?* Now erase anything that you feel has stopped serving your growth. If you have a hard time picking up your eraser even though you feel that you should, let me give you some advice. Do it! Don't be afraid to erase anything else that you've created in your life that may not be serving you.

As you look at the board and see any empty spaces that might be there now, ask yourself: *what can I create here? How can I fill the empty spaces? Do I want to fill them at all?* You have the ability to make the choice. But the powerful point is that you're creating your life and it can look like anything you want, despite the fact that your father may not have been there. You can create every aspect of your life from this moment forward!

Power Seven: **The Power of You**

A legacy begins when an individual decides that he or she wants to break a cycle, or wants to have something of great value to pass along that will benefit those of their line in the future. They start a whole new grounding in soil that is rich enough to sustain a family or community in a new way. It stems from an individual's decision to pursue the opportunity for lasting change, because the old way of being is no longer an option.

We can also create our own personal legacies within ourselves. We do this all the time when we change our minds and change the ways that we respond to the world. That is a legacy of emotional and spiritual evolution within itself. Then it becomes a demonstration. If we demonstrate the realization of possibility, we become contagious. Everybody wants to be like that. That's when it expands to a larger platform and then others want to be a part of it as well. In some cases, we call it celebrity or stardom. But it all started with someone's attempt to build a personal legacy.

When people hear the term "legacy," they tend to picture someone with great wealth, fame or prestige that leaves a fortune for their descendants to enjoy. We think of these people as celebrities, perhaps, who are visible to the masses. But that's not necessarily the case. You don't have to be rich to build a legacy for your loved ones. You don't have to be known by the masses; you can be famous to your son. You can be celebrity dad or granddad.

Your life is that powerful. You don't have to become famous in the eyes of someone else to make your life have meaning. For me, in order to begin building my own legacy I had to leave behind a volatile home life. In other words, I needed to get away from my father to find myself. Some people don't need to do that. But a certain balance must be created in order to begin to build a legacy. The time that you spend feeling like you're going at life alone must be balanced with your participation in creating a world that eases the path toward self-actualization for others. So then it doesn't become about you. It becomes about creating something for someone else that allows you to be a valuable resource.

People who are legends and who build powerful legacies will tell you that, at a certain point, their focus shifted. They began to concentrate on creating something that would benefit others that came behind them. Look at the great legends. Take Mother Teresa for example. I don't think Mother Teresa set out to be a legend. I think she set out to help people understand more about the loving aspect of their own nature. And she was a demonstration for that. Her actions never screamed, *look at me I'm famous!* But through her actions she humbly stated, *look at me and see your self.* That's how legacies are built. You care so much about benefitting someone else that you start living your life in such a way that you shine and illuminate a path through the darkness. This type of living isn't about fickle stardom. It's about longevity; you become a guidepost for the generations to come.

But before you can change things, you have to continue to do the work of transformation. You have to have the courage to recognize that there are things that have been off-center in your life. Until you do, the intergenerational cycle of pain will continue and you'll always go back to thinking thoughts like: *I wonder why I'm doing this? Why am I acting like this? Why is my son acting like this?* The work that we've begun here, and the work that you'll continue to do, will help you to recognize the patterns at play.

Compassion is another tool that we use in our legacy building. We stop beating ourselves up so we can get to the work of transformation. Beating ourselves up will eventually spiral to victimhood. We don't want to go into victimhood and we don't want to feel sorry for ourselves. Compassion helps us ask questions like: *how can I be of service? How can I help someone else?* Legacy is all about helping someone else on their journey because of the understanding that we're all connected. Compassion helps us get clear on things that we need to change in order for the lives of our children to be different than our own.

Legacy begins in the funnel of self-discovery, where we understand that we're forever changing. As we change, we grow more and more into the truth of who we are. That truth gives us the platform to demonstrate those things that we've come to know about ourselves. As we continue to express our authentic truth, we become contagious agents of change and transformation. Because we're forever shifting, this consciousness of demonstration and discovery begins to infiltrate every place that we go. People want to be like us. They want to do the same things that we do. Legacy then turns into a platform to give other people permission to transform into their authentic good. It's like a big oak tree that continues to grow for centuries from one small acorn. Every branch has its own legacy, with the trunk of the tree as its center point.

We all pick up negative assessments of who we are along our journey through life. But it's not the truth of who we are. What many people do this project what they believe are their negative traits on to other people. But if we can catch ourselves projecting our negative thoughts and beliefs onto others, we can begin to ask questions like: *how do I really feel about myself? Do I believe I'm selfish? Do I believe I'm not good enough? Do I believe I'm a manipulator?* Once again, this isn't license to beat up on ourselves. These are just questions for consideration. We should bear witness to how we project onto other people and what we say to ourselves pertaining to who we are. Otherwise, we'll continue in our old patterns and eventually we'll become what we secretly believe about ourselves. This is how so many men end up becoming just like the absentee father they claim that they despise.

What we say to ourselves is our power. What we project onto

others is a tool that actually allows us to look at ourselves with honesty and face the shadow parts of ourselves that would stop us from fulfilling our dreams and leaving a legacy of love and hope for the next generation. As we face our fears, as we grow and change into our greatest selves, those coming behind us will take notice of our every move. Through us, they get to have the example of excellence. We get to show them the way.

Exercise: Project into the Positive

You know what other people have said about you all your life. But what do you say about yourself? Who do you say you will be as a person leaving a positive legacy? What does that person look like? What has he left behind him? Here, we're creating a new image of ourselves to grow into.

_____

_____

_____

_____

_____

_____

_____

_____

_____

_____

_____

_____

_____

_____

_____

_____
_____
_____
_____

_____

Now, you begin to sweep away the debris to find this cosmic shine called you. You've allowed yourself to create an environment where you can use all of your experiences to help you access more of your authentic voice. It's like you go on a deep-sea dive into self-discovery. You go further and further down until it becomes the most wonderful ride of your life. Life becomes exquisite. And, again, we're not talking about a world without challenges. And we're not saying that whatever relationship you may have with your father will miraculously change overnight. Rather, we're talking about reframing and reinventing and remembering that we came down here to be powerful agents of change and transformation, giving everybody around us the permission to do the same for themselves, including our fathers. In this way, we can offer the blessings that we've received on the journey of self-discovery back to them. That's part of the freedom. We're not trying to impose anything on anyone. We're just living our lives the way that we believe is best for us.

We matter. What we say matters. Now that we've gone through some powerful processes of self-discovery, our emotions and past experiences will hopefully no longer hold the same power over us the way they once did. When we come up against our triggers we can ask ourselves: *how does this make me feel now? How does this resonate with me? What does it look like to me now?* We're ready to create something new from our old patterns and beliefs. It's just like how African-Americans in the old days took pigs feet and other inedible meats and made delicacies out of them. We may not eat that way anymore, but get the principle. It's just like taking lemons and making lemonade. Before you get something sweet and refreshing, you have to first you have to deal with the sour taste of the lemons.

Likewise, we now have the opportunity to take those painful things that we've dealt with and begin to use them as fuel for something greater. As we processed through our experiences and changed from one dynamic (or mindset) to a new one, we've journeyed far along the line of mental and emotional integration. We're far enough from the initial sting of our experience to allow the jewel, or the lesson inside the hurt, to come forth so that we can reframe it. Now the experience takes on a totally different life for us and for the people around us. We've actually reinvented, or reconstructed, our past through the power of lessons learned. We finally begin to receive the wisdom of past pain. Your pains become a blessing instead of a curse.

We are farther along the path of understanding because we've gone through the self-discovery process. We've changed enough to understand that life is not all about us. It probably did feel like it was all about us at some points because we had to learn how to heal ourselves. But in the process of getting to where we are now, we have the opportunity to realize that whatever it is that we're creating isn't just for our good. It's for the good of those around us. And that means our fathers, too. Of course, there are times that we have to listen to our inner discernment when it says, *you've healed the past but there's no need to go back to try and heal your father.* That's a hard one. To tell you the truth, I'm not sure if I would've gone back to be with my father if he hadn't gotten sick. If he'd died without a true reconciliation between us I would have said, you know what I did my best. I forgave him. But I'm sure I would've been left with many difficult, unanswered questions.

In deciding whether your healing journey should include your father (if he's still alive and available to be contacted) you must answer this question for yourself: *is his life that important to me? You're not asking: is my life important to him?* That's a question that children ask because they want to matter to the people that they love most. But now we know that we matter because our lives are important to us. So ask yourself: *is being part of his life that important to me?*

Sometimes this process of self-discovery leaves us so changed that all we have to do is go back and stand in his presence. Our own spiritual discernment provides us with whatever answers we still need. Truthfully, we don't know how the healing will come. We don't know how the communication will be resolved. We just don't know. But we know that as we heal, we become the vessel through which our personal and family legacy can continue to re-create itself.

We're not trying to figure out how to do something, how to make this happen. This is just about being. The legacy that we then create will live well beyond us, because those that are coming after us will benefit from the path that we've chosen. They may be our own sons and daughters. They may be the kids living the apartment right next to us. But they see us and they want to be just like us. So if we're not healing our biological fathers, we are setting ourselves up to heal the fathers of the future. If we know that we are healing the fathers of the future, then we are healing the fathers of the past, too—our ancestry, our entire line. And that's the legacy we leave.

Take a Breath

Take a deep breath and tell yourself: *I've done some good work. I'm proud of myself. Now onward and up.*

Affirmation

Say this out loud to yourself: *I'm prepared to live the life I love. I'm prepared to live my best and greatest life.*

Graduation Project

It's time to celebrate how far we've come in this process by doing something fun for ourselves! I want you to go out and do something you've never done before. Maybe it's something you've thought about or wanted to do, but you've never given yourself permission to actually do it. It should be something that you're a little afraid to do. Maybe you've always wanted to coach a little league team. Maybe you've always wanted to learn to sing. Maybe you've dreamed of going fishing with your own son.

Do something that takes you out of your comfort zone. Create something of meaning for yourself that will serve others and have a lasting effect on their lives. Again, it can be anything that speaks to your heart. Doing something new and meaningful will get you unstuck in any areas where you may still experience difficulty. It agitates your mental capacities and shifts your thought process. It exposes you to the great power of interconnectedness and interdependence. You will gain a greater respect for yourself and what you can do for others.

Epilogue

I want to congratulate those of you that are on the conscious path of healing, self-discovery and freedom. It's not easy, but it's the only real path to success and self-realization. When we begin to heal and understand more about ourselves, we get wonderful and surprising answers to questions like: *what's really important to me?* Most of the time when we ask those questions, we find that other people are important to us.

Deep inside, we all have an urge or sensibility to create things that make other people happy. We want to take part in the betterment of other people's lives, too. If you're a son who is trying to make your father's life better, even though he wasn't there for you, you now have the power to create scenarios where you can see him more. You can come to understand him because you understand yourself better now.

There was a time when we were trying to get understanding of ourselves from our fathers. But now we've come to know ourselves on a much deeper level through self-inquiry. And we can pass along our knowledge to him as he moves through his transitions. That's what happened with my father. By telling my father that I loved him I gave him permission to eventually say the same thing to me. That's how we flip the script.

Sometimes it takes stepping out alone. Sometimes we have to stand our ground. It is our voice that calls out the masses. And when I say "the masses" I mean we're calling those things into existence that have an indelible affect on the way we live our lives. We're setting ourselves up for emotional freedom, physical freedom and to love ourselves first. That's what this book has been about. It takes courage to move through the situations that have held us back. It takes patience and integrity. It takes compassion and love. But once we do, we get to choose healthy emotional outlets. We may find ourselves releasing through tears and that's OK. It means that we're able to process our feelings through ways that are going to continue to instruct—and not destruct—our lives. We will continue to build ties of love and loyalty that cannot break.

Congratulations and happy new you.

"I Am" Produced by Ben Dowling

1. America the Beautiful
2. Tapping
3. I Am
4. Love's In Need
5. Summertime
6. Jesus Loves Me
7. A Place at the Table
8. Seasons of Love
9. In Your Eyes
10. Come Sunday

"Rushing Over Me" Produced by Ben Dowling & Karlton Taylor

1. Rolling River God
2. Narrative
3. Great Is Thy Faithfulness
4. Home
5. My Father's World
6. Narrative
7. God Bless The Child
8. I Forgive Me
9. Give Us This Day
10. My Funny Valentine
11. Use Me

Charles Holt Productions, LLC
www.charlesholtproductions.com

www.ingramcontent.com/pod-product-compliance
Lightning Source LLC
Chambersburg PA
CBHW072013060426
42446CB00043B/2427